How To Play Otamatone

A Comprehensive Guide For Beginners To Master Techniques, And Play Your First 15 Beginners Songs

Gareth Windell

Table of Contents

Introduction

Overview Of The Otamatone

The **Otamatone** is a unique electronic musical instrument that has captured the hearts of musicians and enthusiasts worldwide since its inception. Created in Japan by the **Maywa Denki** company in 1998, this whimsical instrument has become a symbol of creativity and playful music-making. Inspired by traditional Japanese toys and the sounds of the theremin, the Otamatone combines the aesthetics of a cartoonish character with the functionality of a musical device, making it an ideal instrument for both children and adults alike.

Brief History And Origins

The Otamatone's design is rooted in Japan's rich cultural landscape, where art and play often intersect. The instrument's name is a portmanteau of "ota" (おた), meaning "to play" in Japanese, and "matone" (マトーネ), derived from "tone." Initially, the Otamatone was introduced as a toy, aiming to encourage music appreciation and creativity among children. However, its playful yet expressive sound soon attracted a broader audience, including musicians and hobbyists looking for a fun, engaging way to create music.

Over the years, the Otamatone has evolved in design and technology, offering various models with different functionalities and sound features. It has found its way into classrooms, music festivals, and online platforms, where users showcase their talents through social media. The instrument's quirky nature and ease of play have made it a beloved choice for beginners and seasoned musicians alike.

The Instrument And Its Unique Features

The Otamatone features a distinct design reminiscent of a musical note, with a long neck and a bulbous body resembling a head. To play the instrument, the musician grasps the neck and uses their fingers to manipulate pitch, while pressing on the mouth at the end of the body to produce sound.

Some of the Otamatone's unique features include:

- **Pitch Control:** Players can glide between notes by sliding their fingers along the neck, allowing for expressive playing styles similar to that of string instruments or vocal techniques.

7

- **Volume Control:** The mouth acts as a volume control, where opening and closing the mouth produces dynamic sounds. This feature encourages experimentation with sound dynamics and enhances the musical experience.
- **Sound Variety:** Depending on the model, the Otamatone can produce a range of sounds, from melodic tunes to quirky, synthesized noises. This versatility makes it suitable for various musical genres and styles.
- **Visual Appeal:** The Otamatone's whimsical design and vibrant colors make it visually engaging, adding a playful element to any musical performance.

Benefits Of Playing The Otamatone

Playing the Otamatone offers numerous benefits that extend beyond mere entertainment:

- **Creativity:** The instrument encourages players to experiment with sounds and melodies, fostering creativity and musical exploration. Its playful nature invites improvisation and original composition, allowing musicians to express themselves uniquely.

- **Fun:** The Otamatone's lighthearted design and easy playability make it a joy to use. Whether playing alone or in a group, the instrument brings a sense of joy and laughter, making music accessible to everyone, regardless of skill level.

- **Musicality:** Learning to play the Otamatone enhances musical skills such as ear training, rhythm, and pitch recognition. Beginners can develop their understanding of musical concepts while enjoying the process, paving the way for further musical pursuits.

In conclusion, the Otamatone is more than just an instrument; it is a tool for creativity, connection, and joy in music-making. As we delve deeper into the world of the Otamatone, you will discover its potential to inspire, entertain, and enrich your musical journey.

Chapter 1: Getting Started With The Otamatone

1.1 Unboxing Your Otamatone

When you open the packaging of your Otamatone, you will typically find the following items:

1. **Otamatone Instrument**: The main component is the Otamatone itself, featuring its iconic shape and design.
2. **Instruction Manual**: A user manual that provides essential information on how to

use, maintain, and care for your Otamatone. It often includes diagrams and tips to help you get started.

3. **Batteries**: Most Otamatone models come with batteries included, allowing you to start playing right away. Ensure you check the battery type and instructions on how to install them.

4. **Strap (optional)**: Some models may include a strap for added comfort while playing, especially during performances or extended practice sessions.

5. **Additional Accessories (if applicable)**: Depending on the model or package you purchase, you may find accessories such as cleaning cloths or additional sound filters.

Before diving into your playing experience, take a moment to inspect all the components and ensure everything is in order.

Basic Components Of The Otamatone

Understanding the basic components of the Otamatone will help you familiarize yourself with its functionality and how to produce sound effectively. Here are the key parts:

1. **Body**: The rounded bulbous section of the Otamatone that resembles a note or head. This is where the sound resonates and is produced.
2. **Neck**: The elongated part of the instrument, which you hold while playing. The neck is

where you control pitch by sliding your fingers along it.

3. **Mouth (or "mouthpiece")**: Located at the end of the body, the mouth opens and closes to regulate volume and sound dynamics. Pressing the mouth while playing allows you to produce various tonal qualities.

4. **Pitch Control**: The neck of the Otamatone has a surface that you can slide your fingers along to change the pitch of the notes. The further you move your fingers from the mouth towards the body, the higher the pitch becomes.

5. **Power Button**: Located on the body, the power button allows you to turn the instrument on and off. Be sure to switch it off when not in use to conserve battery life.

6. **Speaker**: The built-in speaker is located within the body, producing the sound you create. Some models may allow for external

amplification through a headphone jack or
audio output.

7. **Battery Compartment**: Usually located at
the back or bottom of the instrument, this
compartment houses the batteries that power
the Otamatone.

By familiarizing yourself with these components,
you'll be well-equipped to start your musical
adventure with the Otamatone. In the next section,
we will explore how to properly hold the
Otamatone and produce your first notes.

1.2 Understanding The Controls

To fully appreciate and master the Otamatone, it is essential to understand its controls and how they contribute to sound production. This section will explain the various parts of the instrument—specifically, the body, mouth, and pitch control—and how to effectively use them to create beautiful music.

The Body, Mouth, and Pitch Control

1. **Body**:

   The body of the Otamatone is the main structure of the instrument, resembling a musical note. It serves as the resonating chamber, where sound is amplified and shaped. The body is typically crafted from lightweight materials to ensure ease of handling while maintaining durability.

2. **Mouth**:

   The mouth is located at the end of the body and plays a crucial role in sound dynamics. By pressing and releasing the mouth, you control the volume and tonal quality of the notes produced. The mouth can be opened and closed to create effects, similar to how a vocalist modulates their voice.

3. **Pitch Control**:

   The neck of the Otamatone is designed for pitch manipulation. When you slide your fingers along the neck, you alter the pitch of the notes being played. The closer you are to the mouth, the higher the pitch; conversely, the further down the neck you slide your fingers, the lower the pitch. This feature allows for expressive playing styles, enabling you to create glissandos and varied note transitions.

How To Produce Sound

Producing sound on the Otamatone is straightforward once you grasp the instrument's controls. Follow these steps to create your first notes:

1. **Hold the Instrument**:
   Begin by holding the Otamatone with one hand gripping the neck and the other positioned on the body. Ensure that your

grip is firm but relaxed, allowing for fluid movements along the neck.

2. **Power On**:

   Press the power button to turn on your Otamatone. Ensure that the batteries are properly installed, as described in the unboxing section.

3. **Adjusting the Mouth**:

   With one hand, gently press down on the mouth of the Otamatone. This action initiates sound production. The more you press down, the louder the sound will be. You can also experiment with the angle of your mouth pressure to explore different tonal qualities.

4. **Sliding for Pitch**:

   While maintaining pressure on the mouth, use your other hand to slide your fingers up and down the neck of the Otamatone. Start at the base of the neck (closer to the body) to produce lower pitches, then gradually slide

your fingers upward to reach higher pitches.
Try to create smooth transitions between
pitches for a more musical effect.

5. **Combining Techniques**:

   Experiment with varying your mouth
   pressure while sliding your fingers on the
   neck. Try different combinations to see how
   the sound changes. For instance, pressing
   the mouth down more while sliding to a
   higher pitch can create a vibrant, soaring
   note.

6. **Practice**:

   Start by playing simple, single notes to get
   comfortable with the sound production. As
   you gain confidence, begin to explore more
   complex melodies and techniques,
   incorporating glissandos and dynamics.

By understanding how to use the body, mouth, and
pitch control of the Otamatone, you will be well-
equipped to start your musical journey. In the next

section, we will discuss the importance of tuning your Otamatone for optimal sound quality.

1.3 Tuning Your Otamatone

Tuning is an essential step in the musical process, ensuring that your Otamatone produces clear and accurate notes. Proper tuning not only enhances your playing experience but also allows for harmonious performances, whether you're playing solo or alongside other instruments.

Importance Of Tuning

1. **Musical Accuracy**: Tuning ensures that the notes you play are in harmony with each other. If your Otamatone is out of tune, the resulting sound may clash with other instruments, leading to a dissonant performance. Proper tuning is especially crucial when playing with other musicians or backing tracks.

2. **Sound Quality**: A well-tuned Otamatone produces clearer, more pleasant sounds. This clarity helps in expressing musical phrases and enhances your overall performance. When the instrument is in tune, it resonates better, creating a fuller sound.

3. **Skill Development**: Tuning your Otamatone regularly helps develop your musical ear. As you tune the instrument, you'll become more familiar with different pitches and notes, improving your overall musicianship.

Steps To Tune Your Otamatone For Optimal Sound

Tuning your Otamatone is a straightforward process. Follow these steps to achieve the best sound quality:

1. **Gather Necessary Tools**:
   To tune your Otamatone, you will need a reliable tuner. You can use an electronic tuner, a tuning app on your smartphone, or a tuning fork. Each of these tools can help you accurately identify the pitch of your notes.

2. **Power On Your Otamatone**:
   Ensure that your Otamatone is turned on and the batteries are properly installed. This will allow you to produce sound as you tune.

3. **Play a Reference Note**:
   Start by playing a reference note on your Otamatone. A good practice is to use the note **C** as your reference. Press the mouth of

the Otamatone and slide your fingers to find the pitch of the **C** note.

4. **Use the Tuner**:

   Once you have played the note, observe the tuner. It will indicate whether your pitch is sharp (too high), flat (too low), or in tune (centered). If the note is not in tune, proceed to the next step.

5. **Adjust Pitch**:

   If the note is flat, slide your fingers further up the neck toward the mouth to raise the pitch. Conversely, if the note is sharp, slide your fingers down the neck to lower the pitch. Continue adjusting until the tuner indicates that the note is in tune.

6. **Repeat for Other Notes**:

   Once you have tuned the reference note, repeat the process for other notes you plan to play frequently. It's helpful to tune notes in the key you'll be using most often.

7. **Fine-Tuning**:

   After tuning several notes, play a few simple melodies to test the overall tuning of your Otamatone. If you notice any discrepancies, revisit the tuning process for those specific notes.

8. **Regular Maintenance**:

   Tuning should become a part of your regular practice routine. Always check the tuning before performances or practice sessions to ensure optimal sound quality.

By following these steps, you can ensure that your Otamatone is well-tuned, enhancing your musical experience. In the next section, we will explore how to hold the Otamatone correctly for comfortable and effective playing.

Chapter 2: Basic Techniques

2.1 Holding The Otamatone

Proper posture and grip are crucial for comfortable and effective playing on the Otamatone. This section will guide you through the best practices for holding the instrument, ensuring you can produce sound easily and maintain control while playing.

Proper Posture and Grip for Comfort and Control

1. **Posture**:

   Maintaining a good posture is essential when playing the Otamatone. Here are some tips for achieving proper posture:

   - **Stand or Sit Upright**: Whether you are standing or sitting, keep your back straight and shoulders relaxed. Avoid slouching, as this can cause discomfort and limit your range of motion.
   - **Feet Placement**: If standing, keep your feet shoulder-width apart for stability. If sitting, sit on the edge of the chair to allow for better movement and balance.

o **Head Level**: Keep your head level and your chin slightly up. This position will help you maintain focus on the instrument and avoid strain on your neck.

2. **Grip**:

A comfortable grip on the Otamatone allows for better control and ease of playing. Follow these guidelines for an effective grip:

o **Hold the Neck Firmly**: Use your dominant hand to grip the neck of the Otamatone. Your thumb should be positioned on one side of the neck, while your fingers wrap around the opposite side. This grip should be firm enough to provide control but relaxed enough to allow for fluid movement.

o **Use Your Non-Dominant Hand for the Mouth**: Position your non-dominant hand on the body of the

Otamatone, specifically near the mouth. This hand will be responsible for pressing and releasing the mouth to control volume and sound dynamics. Ensure your fingers are positioned to easily manipulate the mouth without straining.

- **Relax Your Fingers**: Keep your fingers relaxed and flexible. This flexibility allows for smooth movements along the neck and helps you to easily adjust pitch as you play.

3. **Finger Placement**:

As you play, your fingers should naturally glide along the neck. It can be helpful to establish a finger placement technique:

- **Use the Pads of Your Fingers**: When sliding along the neck, use the pads of your fingers for better control. This technique helps you achieve more precise pitch adjustments.

- ○ **Practice Sliding**: Familiarize yourself with sliding your fingers smoothly along the neck to find notes. Start by practicing slow movements from low pitches to high pitches, allowing your fingers to develop muscle memory.

4. **Experiment with Angles**:

   The angle at which you hold the Otamatone can impact your playing experience:

   - ○ **Tilt the Neck Slightly**: Tilting the neck of the Otamatone slightly forward can help you see the mouth more clearly while also making it easier to reach with your non-dominant hand.

   - ○ **Adjust as Needed**: Feel free to experiment with different angles until you find a position that feels most comfortable for you.

By adopting proper posture and grip, you will not only improve your playing comfort but also enhance your control over the Otamatone, allowing for more expressive performances. In the next section, we will explore how to produce clear notes and develop your sound on this unique instrument.

2.2 Producing Clear Notes

Producing clear notes on the Otamatone is fundamental to creating beautiful music. This section will provide you with tips to achieve clarity in sound and offer practice exercises to help you develop a strong and confident playing style.

Tips for Achieving Clarity in Sound

1. **Consistent Mouth Pressure**:

   The mouth of the Otamatone is responsible for regulating volume and tonal quality. To produce clear notes:

   - **Apply Even Pressure**: Ensure that your hand maintains consistent pressure on the mouth while playing. Inconsistent pressure can lead to uneven sound production, making notes sound muffled or harsh.

   - **Experiment with Angles**: Adjust the angle of your mouth pressure to find the optimal position for clarity. Slightly altering the angle can produce different tonal qualities.

2. **Controlled Finger Movements**:

   The way you move your fingers along the neck is crucial for sound clarity:

- Slide Smoothly: When sliding your fingers to change pitch, do so smoothly and deliberately. Sudden or jerky movements can cause the notes to sound unclear or break.
- Avoid Excessive Movement: Keep your fingers close to the neck to minimize excess movement. This helps maintain focus on pitch control and enhances clarity.

3. Practice Breathing Techniques: Although the Otamatone does not require breath support like wind instruments, being aware of your breathing can help you stay relaxed and focused while playing:

- Stay Relaxed: Take deep, calming breaths to maintain relaxation in your body. Tension can hinder your ability to produce clear sounds.
- Breath Control: When you press the mouth to produce sound, breathe out

steadily. This approach can help with consistency in sound production.

4. **Regular Maintenance**:

Keeping your Otamatone in good condition is essential for optimal sound quality:

- ○ **Clean the Mouthpiece**: Regularly clean the mouthpiece to remove dust and debris, which can affect sound clarity. A soft cloth or gentle cleaner can help maintain the instrument's hygiene.
- ○ **Check for Damage**: Inspect the body and neck for any signs of damage or wear. A well-maintained instrument will produce better sound quality.

Practice Exercises for Developing a Good Sound

1. **Single Note Exercises**:

Begin with simple exercises focused on producing clear single notes:

- ○ **Choose a Note**: Select a note (e.g., C) and press the mouth while sliding to the desired pitch. Aim for a clean, consistent sound.
- ○ **Repeat**: Play the note several times in succession, focusing on maintaining consistent mouth pressure and finger placement.

2. **Long Tone Practice**:

Practicing long tones can help you develop control over sound production:

- ○ **Sustain a Note**: Choose a note and press the mouth. Hold the note as long as possible while maintaining even pressure and consistent pitch.
- ○ **Gradually Increase Duration**: As you become more comfortable, gradually increase the duration of each sustained note to build strength and clarity.

3. **Sliding Exercises**:

Sliding exercises will help you develop smooth transitions between pitches:

- ○ **Slide Between Notes**: Start at a low pitch and slowly slide your fingers up the neck to a higher pitch, then back down. Focus on maintaining clarity throughout the transition.
- ○ **Use a Metronome**: To develop rhythm, practice sliding between pitches in time with a metronome. Start slowly and gradually increase the tempo.

4. **Pitch Matching**:

Practicing pitch matching helps refine your ear and sound production:

- ○ **Play with a Tuner**: Use an electronic tuner to play specific notes. Aim to match the pitch indicated by the tuner, focusing on clarity and accuracy.

- ○ **Record Yourself**: Record your
  practice sessions to evaluate your
  sound. Listen for clarity and
  consistency, and adjust your
  technique as needed.

By implementing these tips and exercises, you will improve your ability to produce clear notes on the Otamatone, setting a solid foundation for your musical journey. In the next section, we will explore the concept of rhythm and how to develop a sense of timing while playing.

2.3 Understanding Musical Notation

A solid understanding of musical notation is essential for playing the Otamatone effectively. This section introduces you to the fundamental concepts of notes, rhythms, and melodies, providing the foundation needed to read and interpret music confidently.

Introduction to Notes, Rhythms, and Melodies

1. **Notes**:

   Notes are the building blocks of music, representing specific pitches and durations. Each note corresponds to a specific frequency and is named according to the musical alphabet (A, B, C, D, E, F, G).

   - **Staff**: Music is typically written on a staff, which consists of five lines and four spaces. Notes are placed on the staff to indicate their pitch. The position of a note on the staff determines which note it represents.
   - **Clefs**: The clef at the beginning of a staff indicates the pitch range of the notes. The most common clefs are the treble clef (used for higher-pitched

notes) and the bass clef (used for lower-pitched notes).

- **Types of Notes**: Notes can vary in shape and size, indicating different durations. The most common types include:
  - **Whole Note**: A hollow circle that lasts for four beats.
  - **Half Note**: A hollow circle with a stem that lasts for two beats.
  - **Quarter Note**: A filled circle with a stem that lasts for one beat.
  - **Eighth Note**: A filled circle with a stem and a flag that lasts for half a beat.

2. **Rhythms**:

Rhythm refers to the pattern of sounds and silences in music. It dictates how long notes are played and how they are grouped together. Understanding rhythm is crucial for playing music accurately and expressively.

- ○ **Beats**: The basic unit of time in music, beats are the pulse that you feel when you listen to a song. They are typically organized into measures (or bars), with each measure containing a specific number of beats.
- ○ **Time Signature**: The time signature, located at the beginning of a piece of music, indicates how many beats are in each measure and what note value receives one beat. Common time signatures include:
  - ■ **4/4**: Four beats per measure, with the quarter note receiving one beat (the most common time signature).
  - ■ **3/4**: Three beats per measure, with the quarter note receiving

one beat (often used in waltzes).

- **2/4**: Two beats per measure, with the quarter note receiving one beat (common in marches).

3. **Melodies**:

A melody is a sequence of notes that create a musical phrase. It is the part of the music that you can hum or sing, often serving as the main theme of a piece.

- **Phrases**: Melodies are often divided into smaller sections called phrases, which can be thought of as musical sentences. Phrases usually have a beginning, middle, and end, creating a sense of structure.

- **Contour**: The contour of a melody refers to its overall shape as it rises and falls in pitch. Understanding the contour can help you visualize how a melody progresses and how to express it while playing.

4. **Dynamics and Articulation**:

Dynamics indicate the volume of the music (how loud or soft), while articulation refers to how notes are played (smoothly or sharply). These elements add expression and emotion to your melodies.

- **Dynamic Markings**: Common dynamic markings include **p** (piano, soft), **f** (forte, loud), and **mf** (mezzo-forte, moderately loud).

- **Articulation Marks**: These include symbols such as slurs (for smooth playing), staccato (for short, detached notes), and accents (for emphasizing certain notes).

By familiarizing yourself with these concepts of musical notation, you will enhance your ability to read and interpret music, making it easier to play melodies on the Otamatone. In the next section, we will delve into rhythm and timing, exploring how to develop your sense of rhythm while playing.

Chapter 3: Playing Your First Songs

3.1 Song Selection Criteria

Choosing the right songs as a beginner is crucial for maintaining motivation and building confidence. This section outlines criteria for selecting easy and enjoyable songs to play on the

Otamatone, ensuring a rewarding musical experience.

Choosing Songs That Are Easy and Enjoyable for Beginners

1. **Simplicity**:
   Look for songs that have a straightforward melody and limited note range. Simple melodies are easier to memorize and less overwhelming for beginners.

2. **Familiarity**:
   Select songs that are well-known or popular, as familiarity can make the learning process more engaging. Recognizable tunes encourage beginners to practice and share their progress with others.

3. **Short Length**:
   Opt for shorter songs or excerpts. Short pieces are less daunting and allow beginners to experience a sense of accomplishment after successfully playing them.

4. **Repetitive Patterns**:

   Songs that feature repetitive melodic patterns or phrases help reinforce learning. Familiarity with these patterns enables beginners to build confidence as they recognize and play them easily.

5. **Positive Experience**:

   Choose songs that evoke positive emotions or are associated with happy memories. Enjoyable music fosters a positive learning environment and encourages continued practice.

By keeping these criteria in mind, beginners can select songs that enhance their learning experience on the Otamatone, making the process both enjoyable and productive.

15 Beginner Songs With Step-By-Step Instructions

The following are15 beginner songs along with detailed step-by-step instructions for playing each one on the Otamatone. Each song includes information on the notes, phrases, and melodies needed to perform successfully.

Song 1. "Twinkle, Twinkle, Little Star"

- **Notes**: C, C, G, G, A, A, G
- **Phrase**: Intro and first verse
- **Melody**: Simple repetition for ease of learning

Step-by-Step Instructions

1. **Familiarize with the Notes**:
   Before beginning, ensure you can identify and produce each note on the Otamatone. The notes for this song are as follows:
   - C: The first note you'll start with.
   - G: The higher note you'll play next.
   - A: The note between G and B.

2. **Play the Intro and First Verse**:
   Start by playing the first part of the song slowly. The phrase for the intro and first verse can be broken down as follows:
   - **Phrase Breakdown**:
     - Play **C** twice (C, C).
     - Play **G** twice (G, G).
     - Play **A** twice (A, A).

- Finish with **G** (G).
- **Complete Phrase**: C, C, G, G, A, A, G.

3. **Practice the Repetition**:

The melody of "Twinkle, Twinkle, Little Star" involves a simple repetitive structure that is easy to learn. Repeat the phrase multiple times to build muscle memory:

- **Repeat the Phrase**: Aim for consistency in your sound as you repeat the phrase. Focus on maintaining even pressure on the mouth to achieve clarity in your notes.

4. **Combine with Rhythm**:

As you become more comfortable with the melody, introduce rhythm to your playing:

- **Timing**: Aim to play each note for a consistent duration. For instance, you can use a steady beat to help you maintain rhythm as you play.

o **Clapping Exercise**: Clap the rhythm of the song before playing it to internalize the timing.

5. **Adding Dynamics**:

Once you feel confident with the melody, try adding some dynamics to your playing:

   o **Volume Variation**: Experiment with playing certain phrases softer (piano) and others louder (forte) to create contrast.

   o **Emphasizing Notes**: You can also emphasize the last note (G) in the phrase to highlight the end of the line.

6. **Final Performance**:

After practicing the song multiple times, try playing it through in its entirety. Consider recording yourself to evaluate your progress and identify areas for improvement.

Song 2. "Mary Had a Little Lamb"

- **Notes**: E, D, C, D, E, E, E
- **Phrase**: Intro with repetition
- **Melody**: Use of a minor scale for a nostalgic feel

Step-by-Step Instructions

1. **Familiarize with the Notes**:

   Before starting, ensure you can identify and play the following notes on the Otamatone:

- **E**: The starting note, representing the melody's foundation.
- **D**: The second note, creating movement in the melody.
- **C**: The lower note that adds depth to the phrase.

2. **Play the Intro with Repetition**:
The phrase for "Mary Had a Little Lamb" can be broken down into two sections, focusing on repetition to reinforce learning:
- **Phrase Breakdown**:
  - Start with **E**, followed by **D** and **C**: E, D, C.
  - Return to **D**, then **E** three times: D, E, E, E.
- **Complete Phrase**: E, D, C, D, E, E, E.

3. **Practice Repetitive Structure**:
The nostalgic melody of "Mary Had a Little Lamb" utilizes repetition, which helps with memory retention:

- ○ **Repeat the Phrase**: Play the phrase several times, focusing on the clarity of each note.
- ○ **Gradual Speed Increase**: Start slowly and gradually increase your speed as you become more comfortable with the melody.

4. **Integrate Rhythm**:

   As you master the notes, incorporate rhythm to add a sense of flow to your playing:

   - ○ **Timing**: Use a steady beat to keep consistent timing while playing each note. You can tap your foot or use a metronome for assistance.
   - ○ **Clapping Exercise**: Clap out the rhythm before playing to internalize the timing, making it easier to maintain rhythm while playing the Otamatone.

5. **Exploring the Nostalgic Feel**:

   The melody of "Mary Had a Little Lamb" is

often associated with childhood memories and simplicity. To emphasize this nostalgic feel:

- ○ **Soft Dynamics**: Play the piece softly to evoke a gentle and sentimental tone.
- ○ **Legato Technique**: Aim for a smooth connection between notes to create a flowing sound, enhancing the nostalgic quality of the melody.

6. **Final Performance**:

Once you are comfortable with the notes and rhythm, try performing the entire phrase:

- ○ **Full Playthrough**: Play through the piece from beginning to end, focusing on maintaining clarity and emotion in your playing.
- ○ **Recording**: Consider recording your performance to evaluate your progress and identify areas for improvement.

Song 3. "Hot Cross Buns"

- **Notes**: E, D, C
- **Phrase**: Three phrases with repetition
- **Melody**: A basic 3-note melody

Step-by-Step Instructions

1. **Familiarize with the Notes**:

   Before playing "Hot Cross Buns," ensure

you can identify and produce the following notes on the Otamatone:

- o **E**: The highest note in the melody, which gives a bright sound.
- o **D**: The middle note that connects the melody.
- o **C**: The lowest note that serves as the foundation of the piece.

2. **Play the Three Phrases with Repetition**: The song consists of three phrases, each emphasizing repetition, making it easy for beginners to grasp:
   - o **Phrase Breakdown**:
     - ■ **Phrase 1**: Play **E**, **D**, and **C** once in succession: **E, D,** C.
     - ■ **Phrase 2**: Repeat the first phrase: **E, D, C.**
     - ■ **Phrase 3**: Play **E** twice, then **D**, and finally **C**: **E, E, D, C.**
   - o **Complete Phrases**:
     - ■ **Phrase 1**: E, D, C

- **Phrase 2**: E, D, C
- **Phrase 3**: E, E, D, C

3. **Practice the Repetitive Structure**:

   To reinforce your learning, focus on the repetition of the phrases:

   - **Repeat Each Phrase**: Play each phrase multiple times to solidify your muscle memory and clarity of sound.
   - **Gradual Speed Increase**: Start slowly and gradually increase your speed as you gain confidence.

4. **Integrate Rhythm**:

   Adding rhythm to the melody helps create a more engaging performance:

   - **Timing**: Use a steady beat to keep consistent timing while playing. Consider tapping your foot or using a metronome to assist you.
   - **Clapping Exercise**: Clap out the rhythm of the song before playing to

internalize the timing, which can help with consistency.

5. **Exploring Dynamics**:

While the melody is simple, incorporating dynamics can enhance your performance:

- ○ **Volume Variation**: Experiment with playing some phrases softly (piano) and others louder (forte) to create contrast and interest.
- ○ **Emphasizing Notes**: You can emphasize the last note of each phrase (C) to highlight the conclusion of the phrase.

6. **Final Performance**:

Once you're comfortable with the notes, rhythm, and dynamics, try performing the entire song:

- ○ **Full Playthrough**: Play through the song from start to finish, focusing on clarity and emotional expression.

- ○ **Recording**: Consider recording your performance to evaluate your progress and identify areas for improvement.

Song 4. "Ode to Joy"

- **Notes**: E, E, F, G, G, F, E, D
- **Phrase**: Intro with melody line
- **Melody**: Traditional melody recognizable and easy to play

Step-by-Step Instructions

1. **Familiarize with the Notes**:
   Before beginning, ensure you can identify

and play the following notes on the
Otamatone:

- o **E**: The starting note, creating a strong
  foundation for the melody.
- o **F**: The next note, which introduces a
  slight tension.
- o **G**: The higher note, giving the melody
  a lift.
- o **D**: The closing note of the phrase,
  providing resolution.

2. **Play the Intro with Melody Line**:
   The melody for "Ode to Joy" can be broken
   down into a clear and recognizable structure:

   - o **Phrase Breakdown**:
     - Start with **E** twice: E, E.
     - Move up to **F**: F.
     - Play **G** twice: G, G.
     - Go back down to **F**: F.

- Finally, descend to **E** and then **D**: E, D.
  - **Complete Phrase**: E, E, F, G, G, F, E, D.

3. **Practice the Melody Line**:

   Focus on mastering the melody by playing it several times:

   - **Repeat the Phrase**: Play the complete melody multiple times to build familiarity and confidence.

   - **Gradual Speed Increase**: Start slowly to ensure clarity, then gradually increase your speed as you feel more comfortable.

4. **Integrate Rhythm**:

   Rhythm is essential for making the melody engaging:

   - **Timing**: Keep a steady tempo while playing each note. Use a metronome or tap your foot to maintain rhythm.

○ **Clapping Exercise**: Clap out the rhythm before playing to help internalize the timing, which will assist you in maintaining a steady flow while playing.

5. **Exploring Dynamics**:

Adding dynamics can enhance the expressiveness of your performance:

○ **Volume Variation**: Experiment with playing some phrases softly (piano) and others louder (forte) to create contrast and emotional depth.

○ **Emphasizing Notes**: Consider accentuating the higher notes (G) to highlight the melody's peaks and create interest.

6. **Final Performance**:

Once you are comfortable with the notes, rhythm, and dynamics, try performing the entire piece:

- ○ **Full Playthrough**: Play through the melody from beginning to end, focusing on maintaining clarity and expression throughout.
- ○ **Recording**: Recording your performance can help you evaluate your progress and identify areas for improvement.

Song 5. "Jingle Bells"

- **Notes**: E, E, E, E, E, E, E, G, C, D, E
- **Phrase**: First verse
- **Melody**: Fun and festive tune for practice

Step-by-Step Instructions

1. **Familiarize with the Notes**:
   Before starting, ensure you can identify and

produce the following notes on the Otamatone:

- o **E**: The primary note that sets the festive tone of the melody.
- o **G**: A higher note that adds excitement.
- o **C**: A note that creates a transition in the melody.
- o **D**: A note that leads back to E, providing closure.

2. **Play the First Verse**:

The melody for "Jingle Bells" consists of a fun and repetitive structure that makes it easy to learn:

- o **Phrase Breakdown**:
  - ■ Start with **E** seven times: E, E, E, E, E, E, E.
  - ■ Then play **G**, followed by **C**, **D**, and finish with **E**: G, C, D, E.
- o **Complete Phrase**: E, E, E, E, E, E, E, G, C, D, E.

3. **Practice the Melody**:

   Focus on mastering the melody by repeating it:

   o **Repeat the Phrase**: Play the complete melody several times to develop familiarity and confidence.

   o **Gradual Speed Increase**: Start at a slow pace to ensure clarity, then gradually increase your speed as you gain comfort.

4. **Integrate Rhythm**:

   Incorporating rhythm will enhance the lively nature of the tune:

   o **Timing**: Use a steady beat to keep consistent timing as you play. You can use a metronome or tap your foot to help maintain rhythm.

   o **Clapping Exercise**: Before playing, clap out the rhythm to internalize the timing, making it easier to keep a steady flow while playing.

5. **Exploring Dynamics**:

Adding dynamics can make your performance more engaging:

- ○ **Volume Variation**: Experiment with playing some phrases softly (piano) and others louder (forte) to create contrast and excitement.

- ○ **Emphasizing Notes**: Consider accentuating the transition notes (G, C, D) to highlight the song's lively nature.

6. **Final Performance**:

Once you're comfortable with the notes, rhythm, and dynamics, try performing the entire first verse:

- ○ **Full Playthrough**: Play through the melody from beginning to end, focusing on clarity and expression throughout.

- o **Recording**: Record your performance to evaluate your progress and identify areas for improvement.

Song 6. "Row, Row, Row Your Boat"

- **Notes**: C, C, C, D, E, E, D, E, F, G
- **Phrase**: Intro and simple repetition
- **Melody**: Easy round for group play

Step-by-Step Instructions

1. **Familiarize with the Notes**:

   Before you begin, make sure you can

identify and play the following notes on the Otamatone:

- **C**: The starting note that establishes the melody.
- **D**: A step higher than C, adding upward movement.
- **E**: The next note, which adds brightness to the melody.
- **F**: A higher note that creates anticipation.
- **G**: The highest note in this sequence, providing resolution.

2. **Play the Intro with Simple Repetition**: The melody for "Row, Row, Row Your Boat" is structured with simple repetition that is ideal for beginners:

   - **Phrase Breakdown**:
     - Start with **C** three times: C, C, C.
     - Move up to **D** and then to **E** twice: D, E, E.

- Go back down to **D**, then progress to **E**, **F**, and finish with **G**: D, E, F, G.
  - ○ **Complete Phrase**: C, C, C, D, E, E, D, E, F, G.

3. **Practice the Melody**:

Focus on mastering the melody by repeating it:

- ○ **Repeat the Phrase**: Play the complete melody multiple times to build familiarity and confidence.
- ○ **Gradual Speed Increase**: Begin at a slow pace to ensure clarity, then gradually increase your speed as you feel more comfortable.

4. **Integrate Rhythm**:

Adding rhythm enhances the overall feel of the song:

- ○ **Timing**: Keep a steady tempo while playing each note. Use a metronome or tap your foot to maintain rhythm.

- ○ **Clapping Exercise**: Clap out the rhythm before playing to help internalize the timing, making it easier to maintain consistency while playing.

5. **Exploring Group Play**:

   "Row, Row, Row Your Boat" is often played as a round, making it perfect for group settings:

   - ○ **Sing Along**: If playing with others, encourage participants to sing the lyrics while you play, creating a fun, interactive experience.
   - ○ **Split into Parts**: If playing with multiple Otamatones, divide the parts so that different players can start at different times, creating harmony.

6. **Final Performance**:

   Once you are comfortable with the notes, rhythm, and dynamics, try performing the entire piece:

- Full Playthrough: Play through the melody from beginning to end, focusing on clarity and expression throughout.
- Recording: Record your performance to assess your progress and identify areas for improvement.

Song 7. "This Old Man"

- **Notes**: C, C, C, D, E, C, D, E
- **Phrase**: Verses with repetition
- **Melody**: Playful and engaging

Step-by-Step Instructions

1. **Familiarize with the Notes**:
   Before starting, ensure you can identify and play the following notes on the Otamatone:

- **C**: The foundational note, establishing the melody.
- **D**: A step higher than C, adding movement to the melody.
- **E**: The next note, contributing to the playfulness of the tune.

2. **Play the Verses with Repetition**:
The melody for "This Old Man" is structured to be engaging and easy to remember:

- **Phrase Breakdown**:
  - Start with **C** three times: C, C, C.
  - Move up to **D** and then to **E**: D, E.
  - Return to **C**: C.
  - Then play **D** and **E** again: D, E.
- **Complete Phrase**: C, C, C, D, E, C, D, E.

3. **Practice the Melody**:

   Focus on mastering the melody by repeating it:

   o **Repeat the Phrase**: Play the complete melody multiple times to build familiarity and confidence.

   o **Gradual Speed Increase**: Start at a slow pace to ensure clarity, then gradually increase your speed as you gain comfort.

4. **Integrate Rhythm**:

   Adding rhythm will make the melody more engaging:

   o **Timing**: Maintain a steady tempo as you play. You can use a metronome or tap your foot to keep the beat.

   o **Clapping Exercise**: Clap out the rhythm before playing to help internalize the timing, making it easier to play smoothly.

5. **Exploring Playfulness**:

"This Old Man" has a playful quality that can be enhanced in your performance:

- o **Volume Variation**: Experiment with playing some phrases softly (piano) and others louder (forte) to create a lively contrast.
- o **Emphasizing Notes**: Highlight the transitions between notes (particularly from C to D and E) to add to the playful nature of the melody.

6. **Final Performance**:

Once you are comfortable with the notes, rhythm, and dynamics, try performing the entire piece:

- o **Full Playthrough**: Play through the melody from beginning to end, focusing on clarity and expression throughout.

- ○ **Recording**: Consider recording your performance to evaluate your progress and identify areas for improvement.

Song 8. "Are You Sleeping?"

- **Notes**: C, D, E, C
- **Phrase**: Round format
- **Melody**: Easy to memorize and harmonize

Step-by-Step Instructions

1. **Familiarize with the Notes**:
   Ensure you can identify and play the following notes on the Otamatone:
   - **C**: The foundational note that starts and ends the phrase.
   - **D**: A step higher than C, adding upward movement to the melody.
   - **E**: The highest note in this simple sequence, giving a gentle rise.

2. **Play the Phrase in Round Format**:
   "Are You Sleeping?" is often sung as a round, making it perfect for group play:
   - **Phrase Breakdown**:
     - Start with **C**, followed by **D**, then **E**, and finish with **C**: C, D, E, C.
   - **Complete Phrase**: C, D, E, C.

3. **Practice the Melody**:

Focus on mastering the melody by repeating it:

- ○ **Repeat the Phrase**: Play the complete melody multiple times to build familiarity and confidence.
- ○ **Gradual Speed Increase**: Begin slowly to ensure clarity, then gradually increase your speed as you become more comfortable.

4. **Integrate Rhythm**:

Incorporating rhythm will enhance the overall feel of the song:

- ○ **Timing**: Keep a steady tempo while playing. You can use a metronome or tap your foot to help maintain rhythm.
- ○ **Clapping Exercise**: Clap out the rhythm before playing to help internalize the timing, making it easier to play smoothly.

5. **Exploring Harmonization**:

The round format allows for harmonization with others:

- ○ **Sing Along**: If playing with others, encourage participants to sing the lyrics while you play, creating a harmonious experience.
- ○ **Multiple Parts**: Divide the parts so that different players can start at different times, creating a beautiful layered sound.

6. **Final Performance**:

Once you are comfortable with the notes, rhythm, and dynamics, try performing the entire piece:

- ○ **Full Playthrough**: Play through the melody from beginning to end, focusing on clarity and expression throughout.

○ **Recording**: Consider recording your performance to evaluate your progress and identify areas for improvement.

Song 9. "London Bridge is Falling Down"

- **Notes**: G, A, G, F, E

- **Phrase**: Intro and verses
- **Melody**: Rhythmic pattern for easy play

Step-by-Step Instructions

1. **Familiarize with the Notes**:

   Ensure you can identify and play the following notes on the Otamatone:

   - **G**: The starting note that establishes the melody.
   - **A**: A step higher than G, adding upward movement.
   - **F**: A note that adds variety and leads back down.
   - **E**: The final note that completes the phrase and provides resolution.

2. **Play the Intro and Verses**:

   The melody for "London Bridge is Falling Down" features a rhythmic pattern that is easy to play and remember:

   - **Phrase Breakdown**:

- Start with **G**, followed by **A**, then return to **G**: G, A, G.
- Move down to **F** and finish with **E**: F, E.
  - **Complete Phrase**: G, A, G, F, E.

3. **Practice the Melody**:

   Focus on mastering the melody by repeating it:
   - **Repeat the Phrase**: Play the complete melody multiple times to build familiarity and confidence.
   - **Gradual Speed Increase**: Start slowly to ensure clarity, then gradually increase your speed as you become more comfortable.

4. **Integrate Rhythm**:

   Adding rhythm will enhance the overall feel of the song:
   - **Timing**: Maintain a steady tempo as you play. You can use a metronome or tap your foot to help keep the beat.

- Clapping Exercise: Clap out the rhythm before playing to help internalize the timing, making it easier to play smoothly.

5. **Exploring Dynamics**:

Adding dynamics can make your performance more interesting:

- **Volume Variation**: Experiment with playing some phrases softly (piano) and others louder (forte) to create contrast and excitement.
- **Emphasizing Notes**: Highlight the transition from G to A and the descent from F to E for added emphasis.

6. **Final Performance**:

Once you are comfortable with the notes, rhythm, and dynamics, try performing the entire piece:

- **Full Playthrough**: Play through the melody from beginning to end, focusing on clarity and expression throughout.

- o **Recording**: Consider recording your performance to evaluate your progress and identify areas for improvement.

Song 10. "Baa Baa Black Sheep"

- **Notes**: C, C, G, G, A, A, G
- **Phrase**: First verse
- **Melody**: Simple repetitive tune

Step-by-Step Instructions

1. **Familiarize with the Notes**:

   Before you start, make sure you can identify and play the following notes on the Otamatone:

   - **C**: The starting note that begins the melody.
   - **G**: A higher note that adds variation.
   - **A**: The highest note in the phrase, providing a slight rise in the melody.

2. **Play the First Verse**:

   The melody for "Baa Baa Black Sheep" is structured with simple repetition, making it ideal for beginners:

   - **Phrase Breakdown**:

- ■ Start with **C** twice: C, C.
- ■ Play **G** twice: G, G.
- ■ Move to **A** twice: A, A.
- ■ End with **G**: G.
- ○ **Complete Phrase**: C, C, G, G, A, A, G.

3. **Practice the Melody**:

   Focus on mastering the melody by repeating it:

   - ○ **Repeat the Phrase**: Play the complete melody multiple times to build familiarity and confidence.
   - ○ **Gradual Speed Increase**: Begin at a slow pace to ensure clarity, then gradually increase your speed as you feel more comfortable.

4. **Integrate Rhythm**:

   Adding rhythm will make the melody more enjoyable:

- Timing: Maintain a steady tempo as you play. You can use a metronome or tap your foot to help keep the beat.
- Clapping Exercise: Clap out the rhythm before playing to help internalize the timing, making it easier to play smoothly.

5. **Exploring Dynamics**:

Adding dynamics can make your performance more expressive:

- **Volume Variation**: Experiment with playing some phrases softly (piano) and others louder (forte) to create contrast and interest.
- **Emphasizing Notes**: Highlight the transitions between **G** and **A** to emphasize the rise and fall in the melody.

6. **Final Performance**:

Once you are comfortable with the notes,

rhythm, and dynamics, try performing the entire first verse:

- ○ **Full Playthrough**: Play through the melody from beginning to end, focusing on clarity and expression throughout.
- ○ **Recording**: Consider recording your performance to evaluate your progress and identify areas for improvement.

Song 11. "Yankee Doodle"

- **Notes**: C, C, D, E, C, E, D
- **Phrase**: Chorus repetition
- **Melody**: Upbeat and catchy

Step-by-Step Instructions

1. **Familiarize with the Notes**:

   Before starting, ensure you can identify and play the following notes on the Otamatone:
   - **C**: The foundational note, played twice at the beginning.
   - **D**: A step up from C, adding momentum to the melody.
   - **E**: The highest note in the phrase, giving the melody an upbeat feel.

2. **Play the Chorus with Repetition**:

   The melody for "Yankee Doodle" is lively and repetitive, making it easy to memorize and fun to play:
   - **Phrase Breakdown**:

- Start with **C** twice: C, C.
- Play **D** and then **E**: D, E.
- Return to **C**, then jump back to **E** and finish with **D**: C, E, D.

- ○ **Complete Phrase**: C, C, D, E, C, E, D.

3. **Practice the Melody**:

Focus on mastering the melody by repeating it:

- ○ **Repeat the Phrase**: Play the complete phrase multiple times to build confidence.

- ○ **Gradual Speed Increase**: Start at a slow pace to ensure clarity, then gradually increase your speed as you become more comfortable.

4. **Integrate Rhythm**:

Adding rhythm will help bring out the energetic feel of the song:

- **Timing**: Maintain a steady tempo as you play. You can use a metronome or tap your foot to help keep the beat.
- **Clapping Exercise**: Clap out the rhythm before playing to help internalize the timing, making it easier to play smoothly.

5. **Exploring Dynamics**:

Enhance your performance by playing with dynamics:

- **Volume Variation**: Play some parts of the phrase softly (piano) and others louder (forte) to create a dynamic and engaging sound.
- **Emphasizing Notes**: Accentuate the transition from **D** to **E** for a bright, lively effect.

6. **Final Performance**:

Once you are comfortable with the notes, rhythm, and dynamics, try performing the entire chorus:

- **Full Playthrough**: Play through the melody from beginning to end, focusing on clarity and expression throughout.
- **Recording**: Consider recording your performance to evaluate your progress and identify areas for improvement.

Song 12. "Skip to My Lou"

- **Notes**: C, E, G
- **Phrase**: Playful intro and verses
- **Melody**: Fun and easy for beginners

Step-by-Step Instructions

1. **Familiarize with the Notes**:

   Before starting, ensure you can identify and play the following notes on the Otamatone:

   - **C**: The foundational note, providing a simple start to the melody.
   - **E**: A step up that adds brightness to the tune.
   - **G**: The highest note in this sequence, giving the melody a fun, playful feel.

2. **Play the Intro and Verses**:

   "Skip to My Lou" is a light and playful song, perfect for beginners:

   - **Phrase Breakdown**:

- Start with **C**, then move up to **E**: C, E.
- Jump to **G** to complete the phrase: G.
  - **Complete Phrase**: C, E, G.

3. **Practice the Melody**:

Focus on mastering the melody by repeating it:
  - **Repeat the Phrase**: Play the complete melody several times to build familiarity and comfort.
  - **Gradual Speed Increase**: Start at a slow tempo to ensure clarity, then gradually increase your speed as you become more comfortable.

4. **Integrate Rhythm**:

Adding rhythm will enhance the playful nature of the song:
  - **Timing**: Keep a steady beat throughout. You can use a metronome or tap your foot to maintain rhythm.

- ○ **Clapping Exercise**: Clap out the rhythm before playing to internalize the timing, making it easier to play smoothly.

5. **Exploring Dynamics**:

   Make your performance more expressive by adjusting dynamics:

   - ○ **Volume Variation**: Play some phrases softly (piano) and others louder (forte) to create contrast and fun in the melody.
   - ○ **Emphasizing Notes**: Focus on the leap from **E** to **G** for an upbeat, engaging effect.

6. **Final Performance**:

   Once you are comfortable with the notes, rhythm, and dynamics, perform the full melody:

   - ○ **Full Playthrough**: Play through the song from beginning to end, ensuring smooth transitions between notes.

○ **Recording**: Consider recording your performance to evaluate your progress and identify areas for improvement.

Song 13. "When the Saints Go Marching In"

- **Notes**: C, E, F, G
- **Phrase**: Intro with joyful rhythm
- **Melody**: Uplifting and energetic

Step-by-Step Instructions

1. **Familiarize with the Notes**:

   Before starting, ensure you can identify and play the following notes on the Otamatone:

   - **C**: The starting note, setting a steady foundation for the melody.
   - **E**: A bright note that moves the melody upward.
   - **F**: Adds tension and progression.
   - **G**: The highest note in this phrase, bringing a lively energy to the song.

2. **Play the Intro with Joyful Rhythm**:

   "When the Saints Go Marching In" features a lively and rhythmic melody that lifts the spirit:

- Phrase Breakdown:
    - Start with **C**, then move to **E**: C, E.
    - Progress to **F** and finish with **G**: F, G.
- **Complete Phrase**: C, E, F, G.

3. **Practice the Melody**:

Focus on mastering the melody by repeating it:

- **Repeat the Phrase**: Play the phrase several times to become familiar with the joyful rhythm.
- **Gradual Speed Increase**: Start at a slow pace to ensure accuracy, then gradually increase speed as you feel more comfortable.

4. **Integrate Rhythm**:

Adding rhythm will emphasize the uplifting nature of the song:

- **Timing**: Keep a steady tempo throughout, matching the upbeat rhythm. A metronome or tapping your foot can help you maintain the beat.

- ○ **Clapping Exercise**: Clap out the rhythm before playing to help internalize the timing and feel the joyful pulse of the song.

5. **Exploring Dynamics**:

Make your performance more expressive by adjusting dynamics:

- ○ **Volume Variation**: Start softly (piano) and increase volume (forte) as you build toward the higher notes to create an uplifting effect.
- ○ **Emphasizing Notes**: Focus on the transition from **F** to **G**, which provides a high-energy conclusion to each phrase.

6. **Final Performance**:

Once you are comfortable with the notes, rhythm, and dynamics, perform the full melody:

- ○ **Full Playthrough**: Play the song from start to finish, focusing on clear note transitions and maintaining the joyful rhythm.
- ○ **Recording**: Consider recording your performance to evaluate your progress and identify areas for improvement.

Song 14. "The Muffin Man"

- **Notes**: C, D, E, C
- **Phrase**: First verse with repetition
- **Melody**: Familiar and enjoyable

Step-by-Step Instructions

1. **Familiarize with the Notes**:

   Before playing, ensure you can identify and play the following notes on the Otamatone:

   - **C**: The foundational note, starting and ending the melody.
   - **D**: A step up from C, adding movement.
   - **E**: The highest note in this sequence, creating a sense of progression.

2. **Play the First Verse with Repetition**:

   The melody of "The Muffin Man" is simple and repetitive, making it easy for beginners to learn:

   - **Phrase Breakdown**:

- Start with **C**, move to **D**, and then play **E**: C, D, E.
- Return to **C** to complete the phrase: C.
    - **Complete Phrase**: C, D, E, C.

3. **Practice the Melody**:

Focus on mastering the melody by repeating it:

- **Repeat the Phrase**: Play the full phrase multiple times until you feel comfortable with the note transitions.
- **Gradual Speed Increase**: Begin at a slow tempo to ensure accuracy, then gradually increase your speed as you gain confidence.

4. **Integrate Rhythm**:

Adding rhythm will make the song more engaging:

- **Timing**: Keep a steady beat as you play. You can use a metronome or tap your foot to help maintain the rhythm.

- Clapping Exercise: Clap out the rhythm before playing to help internalize the timing and make it easier to play smoothly.

5. **Exploring Dynamics**:
Adding dynamics will bring life to your performance:

- **Volume Variation**: Start softly (piano) and increase volume (forte) as you play the higher notes for added emphasis.
- **Emphasizing Notes**: Highlight the transition from **D** to **E**, then soften when returning to **C** for a balanced sound.

6. **Final Performance**:
Once you are comfortable with the notes, rhythm, and dynamics, perform the full melody:

- **Full Playthrough**: Play through the first verse and its repetition, focusing on clarity and smooth transitions between the notes.

○ **Recording**: Consider recording your performance to assess your progress and refine your technique.

Song 15. "A Tisket, A Tasket"

- **Notes**: C, C, D, E, E, D
- **Phrase**: Intro and first verse
- **Melody**: Lively and easy to sing along

Step-by-Step Instructions

1. **Familiarize with the Notes**:

    Before you begin, ensure you can identify and play the following notes on the Otamatone:

    - **C**: The starting note, which is repeated to set a playful tone.
    - **D**: A step up from C, adding movement and variation.
    - **E**: The highest note, bringing energy to the melody.

2. **Play the Intro and First Verse**:

    The melody of "A Tisket, A Tasket" is lively and easy to follow, making it ideal for beginners:

- ○ **Phrase Breakdown**:
  - ■ Start with two **C** notes: C, C.
  - ■ Move up to **D** and then to **E**: D, E.
  - ■ Finish by playing **E** again and then descending back to **D**: E, E, D.
- ○ **Complete Phrase**: C, C, D, E, E, D.

3. **Practice the Melody**:

Focus on playing the melody accurately by repeating it several times:

- ○ **Repeat the Phrase**: Practice playing the complete phrase multiple times to get comfortable with the transitions between notes.
- ○ **Gradual Speed Increase**: Begin slowly to focus on clarity, then gradually increase your speed as you become more confident.

4. **Integrate Rhythm**:

Rhythm adds a lively bounce to this fun tune:

- **Timing**: Keep a steady beat while playing. You can use a metronome or tap your foot to help maintain a consistent rhythm.
- **Clapping Exercise**: Clap out the rhythm before playing to better internalize the timing, making it easier to play smoothly.

5. **Exploring Dynamics**:

Make the song more engaging by adjusting the dynamics:

- **Volume Variation**: Start softly (piano) and increase volume (forte) as you move to the higher notes to add excitement.
- **Emphasizing Notes**: Highlight the repetition of **E** before descending to **D**

to make the phrase more lively and interesting.

6. **Final Performance**:

Once you are comfortable with the notes, rhythm, and dynamics, perform the full melody:

- **Full Playthrough**: Play through the intro and first verse, ensuring smooth transitions between the notes and an energetic rhythm.

- **Recording**: Consider recording your performance to assess your progress and refine any areas that need improvement.

Chapter 4: Practice Tips And Techniques

4.1 Developing A Practice Routine

Importance Of Consistency

Consistency in practice is crucial for developing skills on the Otamatone, or any musical instrument for that matter. Regular practice helps reinforce muscle memory, enhances your understanding of musical concepts, and increases your comfort level with the instrument. Here are several reasons why establishing a consistent practice routine is essential:

1. **Skill Development**: Regular practice allows you to gradually build your skills and confidence. Each session builds upon the last, leading to noticeable improvement over time.

2. **Retention**: Consistent practice aids in retaining what you've learned. It helps keep

melodies and techniques fresh in your mind, preventing the need for constant re-learning.

3. **Muscle Memory**: Playing an instrument involves physical coordination. Frequent practice helps your fingers and body become accustomed to the movements required, making it easier to play smoothly and accurately.

4. **Goal Achievement**: Having a regular routine helps set achievable goals, whether learning a new song, mastering a technique, or improving your overall sound.

5. **Enjoyment**: Establishing a routine makes it easier to incorporate practice into your daily life, leading to more opportunities to enjoy playing and experiment with new sounds.

Suggested Daily Practice Exercises

To develop a well-rounded practice routine, consider incorporating the following exercises into your daily sessions. Aim for at least 20-30 minutes of focused practice each day.

1. **Warm-Up Exercises**:
    - **Long Tones**: Choose a note (C, for example) and sustain it for as long as possible. Focus on producing a clear, consistent sound.
    - **Scale Practice**: Play a simple C major scale (C, D, E, F, G, A, B, C) up and down. This helps reinforce your familiarity with the notes and improves finger coordination.
2. **Technique Drills**:
    - **Finger Independence**: Practice moving each finger independently by playing short patterns (e.g., C-D-E-C)

repeatedly. This enhances dexterity and coordination.

- **Dynamic Control**: Choose a simple melody and play it at different dynamic levels (piano, mezzo-forte, forte). This will help you gain control over volume and expression.

3. **Song Practice**:

- **Choose a Song**: Select one of the beginner songs to practice. Break it down into smaller sections, working on one phrase at a time until you feel comfortable.

- **Slow Practice**: Play the song at a slower tempo initially to focus on accuracy. Gradually increase the tempo as you become more comfortable.

4. **Rhythm Exercises**:

   - **Clapping and Tapping**: Clap out the rhythm of a song or tap your foot while playing. This helps internalize the timing and adds a rhythmic element to your playing.

   - **Metronome Practice**: Use a metronome to practice playing at a steady tempo. Start slow and gradually increase the speed as you become more confident.

5. **Improvisation and Creativity**:

   - **Free Play**: Spend a few minutes improvising on the Otamatone. Experiment with different notes, rhythms, and dynamics. This encourages creativity and helps you feel more comfortable with the instrument.

   - **Explore New Sounds**: Try different techniques, such as varying pressure on the body and mouth to create unique sound effects. This will help you discover the full range of the Otamatone.

6. **Reflection and Goal Setting**:
   - **Daily Journal**: Keep a practice journal to track your progress, note challenges, and set specific goals for your next practice session. Reflecting on your journey will keep you motivated and focused.

4.2 Troubleshooting Common Issues

As you embark on your journey with the Otamatone, you may encounter some challenges along the way. Understanding these common issues and knowing how to address them can significantly enhance your learning experience. Below are some typical challenges faced by beginners and practical solutions to help you overcome them.

Common Challenges and Solutions

1. **Producing a Clear Sound**

   Challenge: Many beginners struggle to produce a clear and consistent sound on the Otamatone. This can be frustrating and may lead to discouragement.

   Solution:

   - **Adjust Your Grip**: Ensure that you are holding the Otamatone correctly.

Your grip should be firm but not too tight, allowing for fluid movement.

- **Mouth Position**: The mouth of the Otamatone should be pressed gently to avoid muffling the sound. Experiment with how hard you press and find a comfortable position that produces a clear tone.

- **Practice Long Tones**: Focus on sustaining a single note (e.g., C) for as long as possible. This exercise helps you gain control over your sound production.

2. **Difficulty with Pitch Control**

Challenge: Beginners often find it challenging to adjust the pitch accurately while playing. This can result in playing notes out of tune.

Solution:

- **Slow Practice**: Practice adjusting the pitch slowly. Play a note and gradually slide your finger up and down to find the correct pitch.

- ○ **Use Reference Notes**: Play along with a piano or a tuning app to ensure you are hitting the correct pitches.
- ○ **Visualize the Pitch**: Before playing, visualize the note you want to achieve and make a conscious effort to adjust your grip accordingly.

3. **Inconsistent Rhythm**

Challenge: Maintaining a steady rhythm can be difficult for beginners, leading to uneven playing.

Solution:

- ○ **Metronome Practice**: Use a metronome to practice your songs at a steady tempo. Start slowly, focusing on accuracy, and gradually increase the speed as you gain confidence.
- ○ **Clapping Exercises**: Clap the rhythm of the song before playing it on the

Otamatone. This helps internalize the timing and can make it easier to maintain a consistent beat while playing.

- o **Break It Down**: Divide the song into smaller sections and practice each part slowly before attempting to play the entire piece.

4. **Lack of Confidence**

Challenge: Many beginners feel self-conscious or unsure when playing, which can affect their performance.

Solution:

- o **Practice Alone**: Start by practicing in a comfortable and private setting where you feel at ease. This helps build confidence without the pressure of an audience.
- o **Record Yourself**: Recording your practice sessions can provide valuable feedback and help you track your

progress. It can also desensitize you to the sound of your own playing, making you more comfortable over time.

- Celebrate Small Wins: Acknowledge your progress, no matter how small. Celebrate mastering a note or a phrase, which will help boost your confidence.

5. Feeling Overwhelmed with Learning Challenge: With many techniques, songs, and exercises to learn, beginners may feel overwhelmed.

Solution:

- Set Achievable Goals: Break your practice sessions into smaller, manageable goals. Focus on mastering one song or technique at a time.

- Create a Balanced Routine: Incorporate a mix of warm-ups,

technique drills, song practice, and creative exploration in your routine. This variety keeps practice engaging and enjoyable.

- ○ **Stay Patient**: Understand that learning an instrument takes time and persistence. It's normal to encounter challenges, and growth often happens gradually.

6. **Inconsistent Tuning**

Challenge: The Otamatone can sometimes go out of tune, making it difficult to play along with other instruments or tracks.

Solution:

- ○ **Regular Tuning Checks**: Develop the habit of tuning your Otamatone before each practice session. Use an electronic tuner or a tuning app for accuracy.

- ○ **Understand the Tuning Process**: Familiarize yourself with how to adjust the tuning correctly. Knowing the tuning mechanism will help you make necessary adjustments quickly.

Made in the USA
Monee, IL
07 December 2024

72708385R00066